Pearly Everlasting

Pearly Everlasting

poems

THOMAS REITER

Louisiana State University Press

Baton Rouge MM

For Rowan Eloise, my granddaughter,
and for Brendan Galvin

Manufactured in the United States of America
First printing
09   08   07   06   05   04   03   02   01   00
5   4   3   2   1

Designer: Michele Myatt Quinn
Typeface: Sabon
Typesetter: Coghill Composition
Printer and binder: Thomson-Shore

Library of Congress Cataloging-in-Publication Data

Reiter, Thomas.
   Pearly everlasting : poems / Thomas Reiter.
      p.   cm.
   ISBN 0-8071-2542-3 (cloth : alk. paper)—ISBN 0-8071-2543-1 (pbk. : alk. paper)
      I. Title.
   PS3568.E526   P43   2000
   811'.54—dc21   99-055820

The author wishes to thank the editors of the following journals, in which the poems herein first appeared, sometimes in slightly different form: *Appalachia, Ascent, Beloit Poetry Journal, Caribbean Writer, Florida Review, Gettysburg Review, Great River Review, Gulf Stream, Huracan, Illinois Review, Journal of Caribbean Literatures, Laurel Review, Massachusetts Review, Mid-American Review, Midland Review. New Review, Pacific Review, Poet & Critic, Poetry Northwest, Poetry Review, Quarterly West, Raccoon, Rockford Review, Shenandoah, South Dakota Review, Southern Humanities Review, Tar River Poetry, Texas Review, Willow Springs,* and *Yankee.*

"The Saddest Man in the World" also appeared in *Anthology of Magazine Verse and Yearbook of American Poetry,* edited by Alan F. Pater (Palm Springs: Monitor, 1997).

"Piney" and "Creek Walking" (the latter as "Walking the Metedeconk") also appeared in *Under a Gull's Wing: Poems and Photographs of the Jersey Shore,* edited by Rich Youmans and Frank Finale (Harvey Cedars, N.J.: Down the Shore, 1996).

A number of the poems herein appeared in limited-edition chapbooks: *The Zalenka Poems* (Juniper, 1981), *Starting from Bloodroot* (Chowder, 1982), *Time in the Air* (Woodhenge, 1990), and *Prairie of the Universe* (Main-Traveled Roads, 1996).

The author wishes to thank the McMurray-Bennett Foundation for its generous support during the writing of this book.

Contents

Everlasting   1

Ore   2

In the Prairie Preserve   4

The Estate   5

Floodwrack   7

My Grandmother's Saints   8

The Saddest Man in the World   10

The Claim   11

The Bench Mark   13

Dream Coral   16

The Delivery   17

Coal   19

In Drought   21

Ice Fishing above the Dam   22

A Letter from Hispaniola   24

First Gardening   27

Runoff   28

Fine China   30

Leaving a River Town in Early Spring   31

A Farm in Kansas   33

Big Pit   34

Whalers in the Trade Winds   36

Canoeing the Bark River   38

The Garden of Martín Huelva   39

Spiderwort   42

Piney   43

The Air We Breathe, Angels   45

Daybook Entry   46

Yellow Man   47

Stone Ways   49

Making Up Trains   51

Bathsheba, Barbados   53

A Well in Kansas   54

The Day before Opening Day   56

Creek Walking   58

Walking on Moss with My Son   59

The Last Word   60

A Cave in the West Indies   62

The Shed   63

Rag Rugs   64

High Season   66

Creek Fire   67

Late Winter in a Field   69

River Changes   70

The Cassava Women   71

Grimes Golden   72

Everlasting

Dry October, the shallows move
across briary ground
so lightly, slowly, there are
cloud flowers on the bedrock.

On the stream bank, lichen
the color of litmus leafs out
on stones, and in that tough company
here's the pearly everlasting,

each flower head a cluster
of tiny full moons.
Centerpiece in a dry vase,
they will not change all winter.

Look: our shadows keep
the frost on stone-bound lichen . . .
no burden. We bend together,
gathering the everlasting.

ORE

A woman wearing high leather shoes
against mud and the evidence of mules
follows the street called Main Chance,
passing hurdy-gurdy parlors
then the tentground where a circuit rider
in boiled shirt and black linen duster
makes one hand a platform for scripture,
the other a cleaver.

She stops at the one tunnel entrance
closed with crosshatching timbers.
Among hopper cars, cogwheels, cables
of silver mines in the Bitterroots
she has gathered flat stones
as a bench: a vow, a vigil
after shoring failed and the Continental Divide
came down hard on hope. A month ago
all the men but one crawled out.

Wearing flowered collar and hoops of taffeta
with brooch and locket,
she loosens a corner of the barricade
and pushes food in, believing
her husband takes it and not the rats.
She hears him working the vein,
forgives him for not saying
how sorry he is he's the darkness
from which mirrors and coins and utensils
come. And what is she? Sunlit
laundry? Their children tossing a ball?

Voices like a jubilee
of mine whistles and calliopes arise
from the tent services, and Burke, Idaho,

cries, "Glory, glory." A vow, a vigil:
she picks up the burden of a hymn
and passes it into the mountain, afraid
to ask why he won't come home.

In the Prairie Preserve

Hollyhock along a wall, the only
wall in upland prairie, a windbreak
for flowers like red and yellow
teacups or handbells that become
seedpods like tiny wheels of cheese,
and in time tall hollyhock again.
The man who claimed these Kansas acres
and their swale of cottonwood
unfurled a map from the land office,
then piled cairns at the four corners
of bluestem, dropseed, Indian grass:
his to bring under the breaking plow.
But his wife wept for a garden wall
to be set between the westerlies
and the hollyhock standing for Ohio,
so the stone freed from outcroppings
went into house foundation and wall.
The homesteaders' house? Cholera,
1871. Whoever discovered the bodies
on the way to his own claim
dragged them by rope to a markerless
grave (who knew their names?),
then burned all clothing and blankets,
that threadbare smoke weighing on
the wind so it bent the backs of grasses
eastward toward Ohio. Later
he came back from his treeless land,
his sod-roofed dugout, to carry off
hewn logs and roofbeam. Distance comes
to be this local: a Swainson's hawk
in the updrafts that cell by column
build cumulus. No one farmed here
again, the soil too thin and flinty
for anything but prairie grass
and hollyhock along a wall.

THE ESTATE

He steps across a threshold
in the Windward Islands, open air
on both sides, walls of the sugar mill
like staircases, and begins the day
by picking up candy wrappers
from around the waterwheel and stone
rollers. Inside the boiling-house
he buffs copper pot and coils
for the National Trust.

Lately, in tending the gardens
as he has for thirty years, whistling back
at green herons in the mangroves,
he's discovered bones, yesterday a socket
smooth as the bottom of a teacup.
From the Middle Passage to this passage,
they are history no one in the Trust
wants visitors to be unsettled by
as they photograph hibiscus and take in
the vanilla fragrance of spider lily.

What forces thrust the bones up? He knows
men lie hereabouts in unmarked graves,
men hanged for burning the cane fields
because their master would stake runaways
to the ground and slather them
with molasses for the mosquitoes,
would make a runaway shit into the mouth
of another then hold the jaws closed.

He brings the bones home.
What should this groundskeeper do,
tell stories that have come down to him?
His children, teenagers, avert their eyes.

He can hear their voices
as he plants rootstock by a reflecting pool:
they tell him what year this is
and who they are, no matter the dead,
no matter these could be ancestors' bones
coming up among the frangipani
that accent the view from the gift shop.

FLOODWRACK

On old maps, the unknown
bears the legend Here Be Monsters.
Here at a bend in the river,
scrub and brushwood went under,
so the territorial song
of the goldfinch came down
to currents that had gotten away
with the bones of Jesse James.
But what is this today, this
grace and prowess of rose-purple
drawing you into the floodwrack
of Missouri River silt? Years from now,
wherever you are when waters fall back,
you will remember thistles,
tooth and floret and spine, because
where they cannot grow has no
worth. They are elders, healers
who can take themselves lightly,
each flower head appearing as
a tiny pineapple with a fright wig,
because they draw their powers
from waste ground and birdsong.
A month from now, gray plumes
will burst from pods and the wind
will place their seeds all over
these bottoms and in the river
to lodge on islands just coming back.

MY GRANDMOTHER'S SAINTS

They filled my bedroom that summer, propped
on shelves of encyclopedia,
on night stands and a chest of drawers.
When my grandmother put me to bed
she took a holy picture from its place,
and the saint's life became a play in which
she invented voices for good and evil—
all those hermits, virgins, missionaries,
and the emperors who martyred them,
cutting off their limbs and breasts.
"More saints from North Dakota,"
she called those mornings, waking me,
and we opened envelopes from a Sioux
Indian mission. We made room
for patron saints of gravediggers and sailors,
of the blind and those with throat disease.
In the bulletin saints came with, children
wore crucifixes and had dark eyes,
while behind them stood the robed men
who blessed the generous.
In the empty playground one day I found
a pocketknife whose leather sheath
read *multum in parvo*. A booklet inside
showed a boy in his workshop discovering
uses for much in little—blades
blunt and saw-toothed, tapered and smooth,
plus gimlet, chisel, and stylus.
I smuggled the knife beneath my pillow.
That night, lying on my side
and propping my head with one hand,
I kept fanning the hidden instruments out
with the other hand then collapsing them,
while I took in the miraculous life of one
who arrived that day in the mail. Long

after the story ended with a kiss
I took down that saint, who knelt in prayer
to a flaming heart wrapped in thorns.
How could I know that the next morning
my grandmother would put the cards away,
and the children from North Dakota
would never waken me again?
When I set the martyr back in her place
I believed she lived in His Kingdom.
They were in the story, those wounds
I crafted with my new knife,
and the light that streamed from them at death
left the torturer changed forever.

THE SADDEST MAN IN THE WORLD

When the Admiral rose from his knees
in the tidewrack on San Salvador,
the first greenness he touched
was the sea grape you can reach
from your villa's pastel patio:
the glossy hand-size leaves, the clusters
too bitter for preserves. Already
he was somewhere beyond the moment,
dead reckoning with compass and log,
landfall by landfall. When he turned away,
Caribs went manacled under sail
for the gold mines of Hispaniola.
"Not to know this garden
and the constellations of this latitude
makes me the saddest man in the world."
Years in the trade winds would pass
without that knowledge. . . . Marooned
three voyages later on Jamaica,
frail and estranged from glory,
he watched his men collect fallen
leaves of the sea grape dried to parchment,
and on them draw naked villagers
in hammocks and canoes. Here
your morning crew sweeps the leaves
free of history into the fires.

THE CLAIM

At his window in the Stonehill Home
my grandfather invites me to watch
the prairie horizon, looking past
wheat fields and silos to where
once again it's 1887
and a man is trampled unyoking oxen.

I learn how wolves in the Territory
can turn the dead out of new graves
unless homesteaders bury their own
right in the trail. This is what they do:

wagons in a loop ride over that
markerless ground. My grandfather
tells me he's eight and dangling his feet
over the backboard as he waits for
the grave to come around again
and appear from under the wheels.

Why should he sit looking straight
ahead like his parents and sister?
He's clicking off sparks from his
favorite stones, the ones
banded with quartz and flint,
and whistling each time. That stops:

his father calls to him softly,
takes the reins into one hand
then reaches back and slaps his face.

My grandfather's eyes do not stop
looking past the standing grain;
that family is coming here
to settle on their claim. He tells me

he can feel the cheek burning,
right here, then lets go of my hand.
I see those wagons moving in a circle
till the man is packed earth and droppings.

THE BENCH MARK

From the memoirs of Lyman Hayes,
Surveyor General of Missouri

1

Splitting good Missouri slough oak at noon,
16 December 1811, I felt the usual tremor
that clean leverage starts in the earth
magnify, and raising my axe again I saw
terrain come rolling in waves a man's height,
boulders bobbing like waterfowl, whales
breaching and spouting, each tree
a child's wobbling top—at which Zebon,
my apprentice, cried, "The end of the world."

A fault like a rip in taut cloth took us,
along with our tent that held instruments and notes,
which the pit kept when it shot us out on
a fountain of alluvium. As we lay pelted thus
a rift appeared along Providence Lake
and those waters tipped into it, at which
the ground softened, sagged, then propelled us
tumbling upwards in a blanket toss.

2

Our clothing soaked but our limbs sound,
we struck a line toward the Mississippi, fearing
it too had vanished into chasms
and with it the village of New Madrid.
In front of us lay a fissure jagging
out of sight to left and right, uncrossable
until the earth moved again and a cottonwood
rose from that sunken floor, but upside down
so the roots made a bridge for us—

the same tree that an hour ago
I had blazed and marked with bearings.

Below us as I followed Zebon,
the flecks of wave tips. Oh, all I can remember
is that the matted earth gave way. My arms
flew up and then I felt a grip
on my wrist I thought would crush it.
The walls blurred and I was left absurdly
embracing a root two feet above seamless ground.

And alone. Zebon was gone, whom I had hired
on the steamboat landing at New Madrid
when the apprentice assigned me did not arrive.
Zebon, who all that autumn while the valley trembled
had seen wonders: a phalanx of squirrels
surging back and forth through the forest,
massed like passenger pigeons, the river
giving up its dead in enormous boils,
and muskrats changing their nature, abandoning
tunnels and runs where for thirty years
he set traps. No pelts now to sell or trade,
he'd work for me, mastering all our instruments
so the Corps of Surveyors would honor him.

3
When I reached the river bluff,
islands we had charted for navigation maps
stood like buttes above the dry channel
and swift water scoured New Madrid.
The earthquake had taken that famous slough
in which a colony of flatboats, lashed
together, became a dance hall and saloon
that at the sheriff's approach could be poled
to the opposite shore. Love boats,
Zebon called them, and when he came back drunk

14

all our lines and marks amused him.
Perfumed powder floating from
that burst cattail of a beard,
he straddled a meridian and sang "Buffalo Gals,"
hopping from one foot to the other,
then took up the voice of the circuit rider
who climbed onto cypress knees and pleaded for
the souls of trappers, raftsmen, sawyers,
crying, "Forsake these pestilent waters
for the Blood of the Lamb."

Lost minutes of arc and angles of azimuth,
strayed meridians, broken grids.
But I was a young man in the river's
annus mirabilis, so I stayed on,
training apprentices and section by section
running the lines that have given title.

4
Still, that day begins over and over.
Zebon and I awake at dawn distracted,
sullen, for the first time
no words passing between us.
I clamp the transit in place and plumb it,
am giving signals for the leveling rod's
position to set the day's bench mark
when the lens fills with a swirl of shadows—Zebon
mobbed by songbirds! He staggers out of focus,
and when I bring him back, wings beat
against his breast, talons hook in him
so he crosses his forearms over his eyes.

As I keep the cross hairs on him
all the aspects change.
He opens his arms and looks at me,
for the creatures have grown docile, and show
no disposition to fly from that laughing man.

Dream Coral

Where are the stony fractions and iotas
waves lay down along the beach?
At dawn the scavenging children carry off
antlers, fans, and hemispheres of cortex
to be stuccoed onto villa walls
or mixed into the mortar
of Blackrock Asylum you went by today
in the rainbow minibus, no stops
between your resort and duty-free
shopping in Bridgetown.

From this thatched balcony your camera
reads the sea for the right exposure,
but at night breakers you have never caught
wash through your rooms
and through the walls of Blackrock, drawing back
dreamers and pieces of the reef,
tumbling all together. By morning
the children set everything in place again,
and you remember nothing.

There are men and women who know this,
who are not beggars though they reach
through Blackrock's iron gate,
hands upturned as if holding
a passage they've opened to
for your instruction. All day they recite aloud
the journey you took with them.

THE DELIVERY

He had Molo Fuel Co. across his back,
and whatever his name, it changed
the time an overnight snowfall ending
as freezing rain made a chute
of everyone's front steps. My brother
and I on our way to school heard
the minister's grandmother cry out,
"You're the Angel of Coal" to the man
climbing from truck to bin and keeping
a double grip on the rope handle
of a canvas basket on his shoulder.

The rattling tin channel he lowered
through our cellar window gleamed
like a playground slide. There the Angel
taught us about coal: how men
with lantern helmets and black lungs
rode elevators into the earth,
how veins could smolder a hundred years
from lightning traveling through tree roots.
He always took snow and wiped away
his handprints from the window frame.

Mornings, our father stoked the fire,
adjusting dampers and grates, then closed
the cast-iron door whose coiled wire
handle, pinecone-size, bounced ticking
three times and went still. Cheesecloth
tacked over registers to catch the dust
billowed, sailing us into daylight.

Then one day another man appeared
in the Molo Fuel jacket, and wouldn't
say anything. Where was the Angel?

That night listening at the register
between our beds we heard neighbors'
voices rising from the living room:
news our coal man had hanged himself.
His secret was out. Delivering
on the other side of town, he let
a boy climb behind the steering wheel,
gave the kid nickels to touch him.

We learned nothing more about coal,
but still had the endless
clinkers, impurities fired down to heft,
their ridges veined red and yellow
when we blew the ashes away.

We rescued them from the trash
as always, filling coat pockets,
but now on our way to the river
we took turns as the Angel,
moaning and chasing each other,
a temptation of clinkers in both hands
and crying, "Touch me! Touch me!"
Then hurled those failures onto the ice.
Neither of us had the arm to reach
the other side, so they froze in place
till the first thaw took them down.

COAL

After a night of ticking off distances
by water towers with the names of towns,
I pull over above the river.
On the other side, a railyard—
a roundhouse collapsed to its turntable,
on an outer siding a few boxcars
shunted to weeds and graffiti.

I remember the coal fires
kids used to edge up to
beside a freightyard far from here,
listening after dark
between the roundhouse and the river
to men threatening yard bulls
and cursing the sheriff who worked those waters
with grappling hooks.

All that winter
I carried around in my head
the tiny notch and looping line
cut into our gatepost, sure it was a sign
those men would burn our house,
as someone said they did
if your parents turned them away.
Hadn't I once seen a match struck
on a rail and flicked into
a shed of flares?

One time we taunted each other
to meet at dawn and watch
how they hid themselves on an outbound freight.
I woke and dressed before
my father's shovel made a chalky collapse
in the coal bin, before the first

flat whump in the firebox
meant heat would be jetting from the register.

But the men who awakened around fires
and left them banked for others
had already taken the river route.
Nothing was coupling and switching
as we poked into the ashes;
and the coals, when we blew on them,
came back in voices washing over us.

In Drought

Stove-in rowboats crowd a catfish
in the channel's last pool.
Every feeder creek upstream's
a slump of dust, so the fish ends up
a fixture in the neighborhood,
a crawdad in a tin can.
Didn't he teach the river its depths
when whiskers tipped with taste buds
foraged in the bottom silt—
or lateral lines of nerves,
gills to tail fin, picked up
a minnow dying in pickerelweed
and larvae piling tiny stones
for concealment? But now his dorsal's
a flag, and any Izaak Walton
who's made a version of his own hat
out of a sunken stump, flies
and plugs and wobbler spoons,
can plod right in and creel him.

Ice Fishing above the Dam

1

He puts his sledgehammer and chisel
beside the hole rigged with slats
to carry a tip-up, a flag on piano wire
cocked in a loop,

works the bait bucket
deeper into snow against the chance
of wind off Wisconsin bluffs,
lays the gaff on top,
then climbs to a shoreline terrace.

He can see downriver past the lock and dam
to his bait shop, and beyond
to the Illinois Central trestle
where ice jammed against pilings
builds these gorges pilots say
go almost to the bottom.
He looks for signs of thaw
as dark slumps in the level snow.

Fishermen down from Minnesota
tell him the St. Croix is drifted
to the tops of boathouses,
and when all those rivers let go
into the Mississippi
in a late March rain . . .
But today there's only his path
shoveled out to the channel.

2

Something's tripped the flag.
He hauls line hand over hand

and knows it's a sauger—silt
for flesh, bones thick as pine duff—
because it comes up faster than his line
and flattens against the ice.
He edges it toward the hole
by bringing the sledge down lightly
behind the shadowy fish. Gaffed,
its gills freeze open like axe bites.

In his bait bucket are layers
of the cases of caddis grubs,
their spirals, flasks, chimneys
seined from the river last fall.
He thumbnails a circle around one,
slides apart the halves
stuccoed with snail shells,
then runs the white grub onto his hook.

He'll keep taking sauger,
bad bones and all, until he hears the signal
from his shop—the day's first fisherman
sounding the horn salvaged
from the towboat *Council Bluffs*, rammed
by her own barges in a sleet storm.

3
Trash fish?
He pickles the eyes for bass bait
and scores the flanks into trolling strips;
he freezes entrails and air bladders
to grind up for stink bait in the spring.

A Letter from Hispaniola

To Fra Andres Quintana of Seville,
1 October 1500

I am Juan Alvarez Molina, médico
to the Fortress of Santo Domingo.
I write of this world, of these Indies,
because word coming off the caravels
is that you are gathering accounts
of our natural kingdoms to tell our story.

I am no academy's botanist or zoologist,
so bow to you there, though I am *here*
making what notes I can, a beginning
in plain Castilian of what I observe
while ministering to the men. A paste
of resin from the buttress roots
of what I call the wool tree appears
to draw out ichor from stings; a bush
I found in the cloud forest has berries
that when pressed to their essence
—I try each medicine first on myself—
may becalm the roarings consequent upon
eating unfamiliar fruit.
Who helps me understand this world?
Who comes to Isla Española except for
gold or property or politics?

Fra Quintana, write nothing yet
of these latitudes where constellations rise
no one has named. I am reading a treatise
by one Fernando Annari, humanist
at the University of Padua, who claims
a passive prudence in scholarly Latin,
ridicules the notion of journeying here

24

to know man and nature. *Nota bene:*
He made captive Indians paint themselves
(European dyes, of course) and dance
into a simulated ecstasy
in a lecture hall while students took notes.

"The myths and allegories of antiquity
are lamps enough." His words, making this nib
tremble. He interviews sailors,
who for money will say . . . what?
That Indians press themselves to the earth
and eat spiders, termites, worms.
That the shade of some trees is narcotic.
That a fish answering to its own name
ferries ten men at a time. I read
how gold flows in the mountain streams
and gathers inside us. (I have a small
nugget I passed this morning
I would like him to beat into leaf!)

Come to Santo Domingo. We need
your plain habit and sandaled feet.
The ship that brought Annari's errors
carried a royal secretary in taffeta
frills and crimson silk shoes,
ready with ledger to record the fabled
hut of parrot feathers, filled with gold.
Come. Human knowledge and Holy Faith
will be served. You can work to end
the *requerimiento*, that deceit whereby
conquistadors intone a Latin scroll
to Indians gathered in wonder
at the men stepped down from heaven:
"Fall to your knees. Give all your faith
to the Holy Father and the Crown that sent us
or be taken now in chains."

Come. Forest and marshland will be yours
for the setting down of sheer fact
and honest hypothesis—marvel enough.
No one knows what petal or heartwood,
what bees' comb or lizard's gland,
may prove a balm, a curative. Here
we find what Castilians call quinces,
though they are not; birds called pheasants,
which are not; cucumbers, not so.

You can be our Adam, Fra Quintana,
but the world we offer has fallen
like yours to cunning and vainglory.
Prodigies brood in our humid air.
Rumor's a cannonade, and truth
is pollen wafting against armor.
Yesterday a hidalgo, privileged to be free
of the Old World's usurers and footpads,
returned from raiding a village
for its comeliest woman and noised about
—another datum for Annari?—
that by God's wounds he had witnessed
wildfowl of the cordillera lay eggs
from the mere company of capons.

First Gardening

Winter gives over and a man comes out
because he signed for a package his wife
ordered: a froth of praying mantis eggs
it says to plant first in the garden
against the cutworms and aphids of July.
Turning the earth, he surprises
an urgency in himself. Thirty Octobers
he knelt beside her to roll
the chickenwire tight and pull up
cucumber vines. What did she teach him
after they had cleared the earth?
On the stream bank below the garden
he learned the marks of everlasting
pea, lamb's-quarters and, branching above
years of dieback, the herb costmary
for the power of second sight.
He learned how pollen grains in updrafts
grow ice crystals around themselves
and stream away as filaments of cirrus.
The predators are in place, and he knows
what seeds he will have to sign for.

RUNOFF

San Cristóbal, Dominican Republic

Surprised in sunlight by water breaking
against the heels of her shoes,
the child in school uniform turns to look
back along the worn pathway,
past the sugar mill ruins and broken
arches of aqueduct, to the mountain
whose seeds and leaves are flowing by.
The rain has already ended there,
the summit caught in clouds like
her father's gossamer fishing nets.

Wet to the ankles anyhow, she dances
a reggae step, singing, the copybook
and catechism in her backpack no burden.
A vendor selling peanuts and fruit
from a cabinet mounted on a wheelbarrow
claps time, then tells her not to idle,
the other children have already gone by.

Rainwater goes on home ahead of her
into the stone gulley Main Street her family
lives beside. She never wants to move—
all her best friends are there.
But her father calls it Pinchtown
and plays cards on an oil drum table
in Momma Flamboyan's Redemption Rum Shop
when he comes home from deep water,
his arms lit up by the scales of fish.

Meeting his sailboat on weekends, she loves
how a wave in retreat from cast-up
fragments of coral will leave marks

like comets' tails in the sand, the harbor
filling with comets from the sea.
Are they still there? he always asks,
looking behind her, his back to the sea,
frightening her because he means
the roofs of sailcloth and thatch, the walls
made from hurricanes' leavings: signs
for soft drinks, motor oil, currency exchange.

Those Spanish conquerors and their horses
the Indians believed were one
creature, a god from under the sea
—the class read that in a story—
did they ride down from the mountain
splashing along this path? she wonders.
She dances again, then recalls a promise
to help and listens for her name. Her mother
bends to fill a washtub with this flowing.

FINE CHINA

No one gets here by pulling over
on the high plains interstate where
a bronze marker, historical as hope,
directs you to ruts from wagon trains.
Consider the third earl of Anglesley,
who wanted nothing from the overland
trails, their chores and sorrows,
but came here for the buffalo herds,
their fur charring the grasslands.
He had his guides dam the only creek
in this corner of the Territory
and build a houseboat, so although
he lacked companions of his own breeding
he would have joy and ease in the hunt.
Each morning the vaporous ascension
into light, the valet gathering berries,
drovers out to cut part of a herd
past the earl at his nine-chambered rifle.
He once walked out of sight of the lake
entirely on the flanks of buffalo.
He hand-picked their bones for the voyage
into place settings of china,
and to this day guests at Anglesley
praise the purity of the tea service.
Foliage, affinities: there's a buffalo
here on the high plains, waiting
for something to be made of it,
deep in this year and last, in prairie
wildflowers and grasses, their pollen
patterning the fine turns of bone.

LEAVING A RIVER TOWN IN EARLY SPRING

The thresholds of merchants are sealed
with sandbags and plastic tarps.
Residents, roped-off, attend
the record upriver snowmelt flowing
across their macadam on schedule.
All watch the TV crews connect
cables and cameras and establish focus
for astonished inland towns and farms.
The governor's helicopter descends.

Alone, I turn from the curb-
channeled Mississippi and climb
the hill behind the railway station
to watch for the Burlington *Zephyr*
I've dreamt myself onto for years.
From the depot westward a crane
has raised the roadbed onto quarried blocks
a mile through marshland to the trestle
over the river. There my father set WPA
abutment stones going under now.
For a young son then he would tell
stories of divers stalked
in channel mud by catfish
"long as the grave." By dawn
his bridge will go under with the others.

On the opposite bank the daylight
boxcar burliness of the Shoreline Inn
thins and grows dim against water
that will crest tomorrow at its eaves.
I entered that tavern with my father once,
while his high labors were making
the trestle worthy, and among the roaring
workers from the annual circus

he spoke to other men, to those who carpentered
Pullman cars in the roundhouse.

The switchyards are flooded now
where kids used to trail bums on their way
to parish refectories and mission cots.
I remember the winter day one of them
turned to face us on a siding. He was the one
we called Apples because the first time
we saw him his long coat was knobby
from an orchard up the line.
Was it because the yard bulls
had beaten our town's name into him,
or was it to teach us a lesson
that now in a single motion
he dipped to the rail and came up
spurting a wooden match? He snapped
that particle of grace and rage
into high weeds beside a Railway Express
shed, then dropped down the bank
to the frozen river. I remember
there wasn't a late winter thaw
when the sheriff's grappling hooks
didn't bag John Doe for a county grave.

The *Zephyr* curves toward me from the trestle,
though it slows where marshy inlets a mile apart
connect across the rails
and the conductor wades ahead to check
for washouts. I am setting out
from the river my father set stone on stone
to pass over and Apples lost us on.

A Farm in Kansas

If a riverbed over time
changes by oxbow and undercut,
where am I now? I've gone out
onto river ice, every step
held on its way to the ocean.
Suppose someone came before me.

The blizzard of 1871—suppose
a homesteader building cairns
to mark off his claim
wandered lost in the whiteout
and saved himself by carving his way
into the carcass of a buffalo.

For three days, in place
of entrails, a man praying!
I am saying this to make a shelter
for us both where he crawled from
bones onto land that in his lifetime
lost its way in water,

where he set foundation stone
with the oils and salts
from his hands. No need to
look to one bank, then the other.
My weight is nothing. I'm here
for the time the river gives me.

Big Pit

We stepped from the cage lift into coal,
and a sound was already there. I looked
my helmet beam down wooden trussing
onto the weather of Wales runneling
on either side of us, its color
leached from tailings, bones, fallen leaves.

Tunnels out of history, the first in Powys,
our guide began, but now shut down
by drilling in the North Sea. Only a few
colliers like himself came back each day
to Big Pit Museum.

Then the pony stalls, a name on each
and a harness hanging from a nail.
The Shetlands last drew hopper cars
fifty years ago, and he knew them all.
Summers they were led above ground,
and we should have seen them
running across fields, flowers in their hoofs.

Where else would boys from slagtip valleys
go but into the mines of Wales?
Pickaxe, shovel, auger like an oversize
brace-and-bit, a powder keg at each cut.

But the first work in their apprenticeship
was to watch a kerosene lantern's
flame for the deepening blue clarity
of methane or carbon monoxide.
And then how they'd ring bells, racing
along every coal face.

Where the tunnel branched he said
he would show us a place we could never

find again, so he touched our helmets dark
until we were there. The last went out
and nothing came back. Pure absence.

Or presence. I thought of those boys,
their lives all flame and ancient forest
and none of it of their making,
their songs and games gone into seams
for others after them to mine.
And now no others, only us
playing at darkness. Someone spoke.

Lights appeared and our collier
led us farther in. He gave us depth,
tonnage, and at the haulage engine
that had emptied the pony stalls
for good but kept the children,
spread his arms wide to barely take in
one of its minor gears.

"Whaling station ruins," our map reads,
but in the Windward Islands?
We come to a cove of black sand
where a sailboat's beached on wooden skids,
windlassed above the surf.
The White Wing, freshly caulked.
"We're the ruins," a voice calls from
a stone building half-hidden by sea grapes.
"Twin brother's coiling harpoon line."
A straw hat appears above the gunnel,
then drops back. "He's Aython MacKenzie,
I'm Oliverre, and this place? Not New Bedford."

He waves us into the station. "Scots?
you're thinking. You see flowing white hair,
a face look like a knot in wood, so
you wonder what kind of mix we are."
Kettles and pipes, knives, cutting floor
gapped for drainage, and in a corner
barrels for the oil perfumed with limes
islanders burn when the power's down—
he quicksteps through the operation.
"More than one churchgoing matron
she laces up our famous bone stays,"
he adds. "Everybody pays in barter.
Barter too for MacKenzie's Baleen
Delicacy. What it tis? Give meat
a long soak in jackiron rum
for breaking fibers down, then smoke it
black as this volcanic beach."
He grins. Come back in a week and they'll
make an exception, take American cash.

A MacKenzie fifteen generations back,
we learn, was a shipwright and whaler,

one of the Shetland Islanders who lost
their patrimony, their boats and homesteads,
to English godliness and English axes,
then found themselves "Barbadosed"
to build inter-island schooners.
They fled in the first one launched,
scuttled it on the reef beyond this bay,
and swam ashore to build whaling stations
along the coast. Oliverre points
to the cloud forest. "Boatman's oak.
Three hundred years those branches carry
the right curve for ribs. We framed out
The White Wing forty years ago."

We follow as he greases the tracks
with a flyblown piece of fat
while Aython waits to run up sail.
"We never lose to sharks," he says.
"We go bind the whale's jaw with rope
so that beast won't sink and drag. Times
we sail back with only our own wake
in tow, jackiron does for body and soul."
He hoists himself over the gunnel,
unclips the windlass cable, and now
the last whalers in the Windward Islands
cast off. We keep pace to where breakers
churn coral fragments. He calls back,
"Our sons all work in tourist hotels.
Tell me where is the memory in that."

CANOEING THE BARK RIVER

Did our shoulders ever tighten like this
when we sculled in college?

Fallen cottonwoods define the pools
brightening toward dawn,
but trees come down in other ways
this early spring, changing the river,
and as we paddle we tear a gauze of pollen.

A sandhill crane's *kur-oo, kur-oo*
draws our binoculars to the straight line
of neck and legs, the long sailing
into level light reddened by clouds,

and when we come back we're floating on
the glint of new pennies, a brass band,
and our paddles, look, they're coated
with dazzling granules. Remember

the summer we waded into fireflies
and swatted the yard to darkness? No,
not darkness, with always one more
rising out of the damp grass ahead,
though the wiffle bats on our shoulders glowed.

It's journeywork we learn as we go,
this deep stroke and feathering
that brings the odor of humus up in swirls.

for Ron Ellis

THE GARDEN OF MARTÍN HUELVA

ca. 1520, the Leeward Islands

1

Atop a mangrove tree, the captain
of the *Lérida* empties a pelican nest
for the crossbows of his mariners.
The young he hurls on their first flight
are not ready, but a true eye
takes them before they fail,
no quarry for the baying hounds.

Last night a squall took the caravel's
heading and set her masts afloat.
Dawn, hopeless of anchorage at
this island—blank sea on the chart—
the crew tracked a wave coming in
from the horizon and lifted their voices,
"In protectione Dei." It lifted the ship
over the reef and careened her
onto black sand and pumice stone
two hundred paces from the sea.

2

A man gets up from the shadow
of the keel. He is Martín Huelva
the caulker, a man of pitch and oakum.
For his service to Santo Domingo
he dreamt of a royal patent to an island,
a small one among the thousands,
its pineapple, maize, cassava,
sons' patrimony. And his grave there
honored. But last night in the wind

he heard bells, flutes, tambourines,
and wept for his children in Seville.

He turns from the mangroves
and their prop roots like rigging, climbs
a gully of gray stones where lava
vaporized a river, where sudden rain
vanishes into the porous bed.
How many times he met friars laboring
along mountain trails in Hispaniola,
skirts and scapulars on their way
to swap the sacraments for gold
masks and combs and amulets.
"Am I the one to judge?" Martín Huelva
cries aloud, then crosses himself.

3

The cries of pelicans and the bowmen's
laughing and wagering follow him.
At first the Indians paddled
singing to greet the Men from the Sky
—even a caulker is one!—
offering parrots and skeins of cotton.
Now they go in flight among the islands,
guided by stars and seamarks
the Spaniards have begun to learn.

Those clouds stacked on the horizon,
do they mark a landfall? Among fumaroles
at the crater's rim he finds a bush dripping
from arrowhead leaves, and once again
marrow falls from the broken bones
of Indians chained to grids above a fire:
a lesson given by Men from the Sky
when the *Lérida* and her hounds returned
with fugitives from the gold mines.

4

The clouds move, the waves have nothing
to break upon but themselves.
A *Salve Regina* ascends
from men kneeling on the black sand.
How many times did the *Lérida* sail
because his labor made her worthy?
He tries to number them, the air sulfurous.

Of the first voyage he remembers
a delirium when the trade winds failed,
the caravel becalmed off Mariagalante,
her leg irons filled. . . . He was home,
he was over the side and halfway down
the Jacob's ladder, weeping and praising
because the sea was a green field
in Andalusia where his children played,
when shipmates took hold of him
and drew the dreamer back among them.

SPIDERWORT

Blue oval petals and gold stamens
where she kneels in Kansas—
so few flowers to claim a prairie with.
She tends them for their brilliant
irrelevance to sloughgrass twisted
into logs for her cooking stove,
tends them because neighbors tell her
how the grasshoppers come, eating
everything plows turn the earth for,
and then the handles of the plows.
It's a child's game but means Ohio
to her: she touches a flower cluster
so it shrivels to a fluid jelly,
becoming its other names. She remembers
a song her mother taught her, beginning
"Oh cow slobbers, maiden's tears."
Does this song come back to her now
so that when she steps into the familiar
rhythm of well and root cellar
she will turn away? Her husband
has finished breaking tallgrass prairie
for the day, 10,000 years unfurling.
When he finds her singing on her knees
what can he do but sweep her up
in a dance step? No matter
he has never done that before.
"Just breathe in the odor of plowed earth,"
he croons. "Just look at the flowers."

PINEY

One day towing a fishing shanty
from lake to lake across a bewilderment
of rivers and marshes in the Barrens,
you find him. He knows you first
by your Ski-Doo, then
by your license pinned like a security pass.

He got here by forcing a foot route
through scrub pine and pepperbush.
He's running traplines and crossbow fishing
always now on posted land—
why else would anyone be
a tenth-generation Piney?

Spring to fall he works wild cranberry bogs,
and when he climbs into waders
to steer a thresher like a garden tiller
bobbing on pontoons, you'd want to be him
just to make that water blaze
and vacuum it black again.

Ask the way back and he'll tell you
where the last narrow gauge
of the old Pine Barrens Railroad lies
that hauled bog iron for Union shot,
or the site of ponds so rich in tannic acid
any one might stare you down
with the face of the Jersey Devil, that
thirteenth child of a thirteenth child,
drowned at birth.

Right now you're merely
someplace between Speedwell and Tabernacle
where springs and currents keep the ice

thin enough for arrows.
He cocks the crossbow and releases line
spooled at his waist. He knows how any April
the cross hairs of surveyors
could sprout from landfill,
how midges could be sawdust dancing on a plank
as a ripsaw passes through it.

THE AIR WE BREATHE, ANGELS

The whole day gone into worksheets
and no poem to speak of—
some clouds the color of tent caterpillar webs,
a man standing on a docking float,
its Y-shape chafing the ice—and now
there's light playing across your bedroom wall.

An hour ago, in the middle of the story
I was reading you, about a runaway boy
lost and trying to tear loose
from a cold scolding of spiny underbrush,
you asked what caused the snowy light
under the covers each time
you moved, and did it mean you'd have to
stay in one place forever.

Fibers and the dry air.
I find you pulling the blanket
rigid with your teeth, your arms
and legs making angels, your body
lit by crystals.
                        Next to that,
what is it to sit up the rest of the night
writing this?

Daybook Entry

Getting down to gather Indian pipes
for their brown stems and ornamental
bowls tamped with spore dust,
I remember how they looked
one summer day we had chosen sides
so war could begin in the woods.

Crawling for clearer aim
through deep shade, I found them
rising around me without
name or use, their stalks
and downcast flowers a corpse white
speckled with leaf mold,
while a BB gun assault
ticked in the leaves above me
and voices volleyed,
"You're dead! You're dead!"

Today these make fit company
for dried zinnias and the velvet
staghorn of the sumac,
but before I go I will get down
how a boy takes cover in the Indian pipes.

Yellow Man

Collecting shells in the riprap
that churns then goes calm between waves,
I watch him go by. I can't tell
his age. He walks along the tidewrack,
past vendors weaving animals and hats
out of palm fronds, past boys from town
playing beach cricket, who simply
pause, holding their positions.

He's turned out in a dozen tones
of yellow, right down to painted shoes,
cane, pipe stem and bowl (you can see
the brushstrokes). For whose amusement?
What thought and feeling go into this?
He's arrayed in the brightness
of allamanda, acacia, chalice vine.
And hibiscus—they live a single day,
and I've seen their petals pressed to fingertips
for shining shoes in the best hotels,
"Yellow Bird" whistled as accompaniment.

I don't know if he can hear me
over the surf and the cries of children.
When I comment on the sea or sky
he strikes a wooden match
dipped to its head in what looks like
pollen, puffs, and continues on,
straw hat pulled down, sunlight
on the worn cloth across his back
swimming like pats of butter.

He lets the day go on without him.
I imagine him entering the kind of house
the tour bus passes on every route,

rain forest or cactus flats,
its whole unplumb improbability
built up from packing crates,
driftwood, old advertising signs,
and roofed with thatch or rags.

I never blame him that he appears
in dreams. I'm swimming beautifully, all
the strokes, when he stops to light his pipe
then steps over a breaking wave
right into the glossy water,
not looking away, not going home.
He's about to speak—A question?
Some wisdom I can live by?—
when he disappears, leaving
amber-to-orange flowers floating everywhere
and a cold current at my groin.

STONE WAYS

The way boggy in matgrass and heather,
then firm in a lashing of yellow gorse
the last half-mile to the church
called St. Ogdal's in the guidebook.
That Welsh hermit in his wanderings
raised the original of mud and wattle
in praise: where he fell in prayer
when robbers set upon him, the legend
says, a stone outcropping opened
and folded gently around him.

The traffic bound for seaside pavilions
stays almost out of hearing.
No one comes who is pilgrim enough,
who isn't shut out from stone
by more than locks and hazard signs,
but I find a window where sunlight
through the fallen transept is enough:
the altar's that haven stone itself,
though now it holds a steeple bell
carried off by Vikings after the saint's death
and retrieved by angels. The penitent
cured of demons, lesions, unfruitfulness,
kneeling there heard it ring.

Those clouds darken, may come this way.
I give St. Ogdal's a last look,
and someone is looking back.
On a half-collapsed wall of the chancel
a doom figure stands, himself
in ruins, his hourglass broken.
He meets my gaze so mildly,
so out of character, I can't help
this leap: he wants to throw back his hood

and live in the world without cautioning it.
He can't recall the last healing,
and isn't deaf. He wants to be told
what keeps him here when everyone
goes back the way they came.

Making Up Trains

The center span trembles on its pile,
pivoting. From his clapboard station
above the gears and great cogwheel,
the bridgetender sights along rails—

a level arc over switchyards
and across ice to the channel,
where the towboat *Shelly Mott*
holds her barges against the current.

A patrol launch waits to haul in
lighted buoys from sandbars
bossing the Mississippi.

Two thousand openings ago, the river
crested an arm's length below these ties,
but tonight the wind will set channel ice
in a fine grain and give him
silence enough for his own voice.
He logs the last coal tonnage through

and locks back on the roundhouse, its roof
fallen, that sometimes he can stop himself
from looking into, where for thirty years
in shops along the turntable's rim
his men built sleeping cars.

The famous trains of the valley route
were made up here
between the roundhouse and the river—
on sidings he calls the Rip Yards

because his first winter at the trestle's hub
his old apprentices learned

to retool the *White Wing* and *Wapsipinicon*
for freight or mail.

Then too much rolling stock
came back, so Pullmans lit the ice
and the rip crew salvaged iron from char
left on a spur for the next flood.

Is it this way a man's craft
goes on from him?
Checking linkages and ties before
the next freight can be cleared across,
he knows what a carpenter knows

when timbers of the roundhouse roof
lie on the turntable, star-shaped
like the business end of a bit.

Bathsheba, Barbados

I get off the bus whose grand loop
the driver tells me over calypso carols
from the Voice of the Windward Islands
will bring him back, don't worry.

Walking the beach below palms
twisting in the trades,
I stop to retrieve in a wave's lull
the half-buried skull of a fish.

Formed like a shield, the underside
bears an abstract figure of raised bone,
cowled and with arms outstretched.
I have been to the duty-free shops
that sell these, shellacked and mounted,
art and nature conjoined in
"a curio worth possessing."

Before bells rang under crosses
on this side of the sea
the soldiers of Ponce de León
beached their longboats here.
Streams, vines, a new light on earth,
and royal patents to collect souls
for plantations of sugarcane.

What is that in the wind?
Because the Spaniard killed their king,
Carib warriors hang themselves
in groves along the coast

and will not go with us,
though stop by stop the festive bus comes on.

A WELL IN KANSAS

No need to show fields of ruined wheat.
Books, a leather harness, overalls,
lie in shreds around the well
these homesteaders dug alone, he
pickaxing soft limestone luckily
the whole way to a steady vein,
she working the windlass to pour out
stones, the two of them creating
the deepest place in their lives.
They pose in clothing they've had to
unpack from a cedar chest: taffeta
with embroidered cuffs, a brooch
at her throat; his silk vest, cravat.
The cloud of mandibles and wings
moved on from here a week ago.
The photographer? He climbed down
from a Kansas Pacific Pullman,
his job to document the dream
for fliers handed out back East
by the railroad's land promoters:
a swale of sloughgrass for sod walls,
a cottonwood grove as windbreak.
But finding every stalk and leaf
gone, he waited in his darkroom wagon
for a direction to suggest itself.
Then these two calling to him.
Crouching beneath the camera's hood
and moving the bellows, he wonders
how he'll be paid. Husband and wife
stand facing each other at a distance
that with one step would be an embrace.
Now? The sodbuster tips a bucket
freshly drawn, and for the time
the shutter needs to reach beyond

August 23, 1874—the light
is good, the shadows not out of place—
glinting like ice chips or honed edges,
grasshoppers pour into her cupped hands.

The Day before Opening Day

I ease my knapsack to the ground
beside some posted woods, unfold
hackle, thread, and hooks
where hatchery trucks could never make it
and the rainbows are real.

You've promised not to let the creek
out of your sight, so while you snap a path
through bankside tiger lilies,
their dry stalks fletched like arrows,
I seine the gravel bottom, bringing up
the morning's hatch in hellgrammites
and the brittle cases of caddis worms.
I match them, dry fly and streamer.

Meanwhile those watchful empty stems
have stopped saying anyone's there.
I pick up signs where the woods begin.
White as stones in the cold riffles
I overturned for larvae, there's
a patch of flowering bloodroot
you went through to break your word; then
a few bruised lavender hepatica, on one
what has to be a fingerprint;
deeper, a stump of loblolly pine,
its green cup lichen tumbled off; no sound
of water now—a mushroom blackened by the cold,
its cap broken, its ripe spore raided,
might be the angel of death.

Each bloodroot bud is furled
in its one pale leaf
when you strike the creek at dark
and I'm here, tomorrow's midges and nymphs

packed up. What is there to say?
I see on your back
the moon hunched like a knapsack.

CREEK WALKING

1

Soon there'll be a March day
like a double agent,
playing the blue anemone off
brown umbels of Queen Anne's lace,

but today the only open water
is thin bands around cattails,
so we trust ice with our weight.

2

You bend to snap off a stalk
because the burst flower sprayed with acrylic
will make a centerpiece—
and suddenly we are on our knees
watching pincers moving armor plate
from the bottom into the light.

Look: in the seed heads of cattails
the backs of stone flies crack open
onto ginger wings and what passes
for the afterlife.

3

Wherever we walk, empty-handed,
they are coming down out of the air.
They stipple eggs onto stalks, each
in its ring of water

widening to let us in.

WALKING ON MOSS WITH MY SON

We leave green footprints filled with stars
in the overnight snow. Zero:
your birthday field guide places us
by Peosta Slough, starting a life list
of the tracks of animals and birds,
deep in winterkill. No fisherman
has come before us to sway in his tracks
on the stiff rosettes of star moss.

Today the channel cat are buried
up to their dorsal fins against
the lowering overcast of ice;
not even blood bait could get them
to trip the flag on a tip-up.
You flatten against the slough,
hands cupped to your eyes, but tell me
it's the carnival and you're looking through
the scratched and muddy coffin
of the Himalayan Man. Taking your place,
I see leaves on a sunken alder
schooled up like shiners.

Junco, meadow vole, quail—
in thickets stripped of seeds we call out
the sure ID's. We are getting down
what passes here for life, step by step
getting down to star moss.
Together we sway between earth and page.

The Last Word

The Oregon Trail, 1851

This is why I was born,
a man tells himself, leaving
a mill town in Missouri for
the Willamette Valley's orchard plots.
His wife learns the wagonmaster's law:
leave behind whatever's not worth
a dollar a pound. The first day ends
at a campsite in Kansas filled,
this mild spring, with anemones—
wind flowers, their white caps
trembling on tall stems.

Children running through the flowers
are currents turning within
the prairie's one motion. Wind
comes from the route ahead
and the rest of overlanders' lives,
the apples, cherries, plums.

Full summer. Where the anemones
and children were that first day,
the seeds of porcupine grass
with their tightly spiraled tails
vanish into the earth by turning
one way in sun, the other in rain.

A thousand miles to the west,
a man and woman have left their only child
under a cairn and crucifix.
How could their daughter have fallen
beneath the oxen while her father
held the reins? Lying together

this first night, the other wagons voiceless,
they watch how moonlight covers
the sand hills drifted along the Platte . . .
Come on, their daughter shouts,
and so they all climb
onto the sled that had to be left behind
in the reckoning of weight and worth,
then close their eyes tight against the wind.

A Cave in the West Indies

You have to extend yourself
beyond belief, the mountain coming apart
in slick chips underfoot
till you reach a terrace above the sea.
Here a vowel of shadow glimpsed
through tamarinds is the entrance
to Arawak dreams and visions.
You find yourself beneath a blue vent
in the smoke-darkened ceiling. Carved
on the smooth walls, deities
of harvest, the hunt, and childbirth
flared once in light from the breast-
plate of the Spaniard standing
where you are now, and were lost.
They did not go with the Arawaks
into the gold mines of Hispaniola.

What this has to do with you
is the purest water on the island.
The mountain's core is a waterfall,
and the river scouring its channel
past hideaway villas far below
pools first in this cavern floor.
You bend to the surface, and what
is this? A face in feathered headdress,
its mouth and eyes deeply shadowed.
A flick of attention tells you
it's a god on the wall, a petroglyph
like those vivid and desirable
batik patterns in the shops.
You cup your hands over and over
then start back down the mountain
that gives this river its bright velocity.

The Shed

Grains of the roofing stick to him,
but he won't say where he's been.
He can see with his father's binoculars
that no one looks up to find him
on this high terrace behind the house.

He can focus on men in orange vests walking
the length of a tow of coal
and staying in place on the river.
He can lie on his back reading *Boy's Life*.
All summer the shed roof is where
things never happen for the last time.

Today the kids next door are watching
cartoons. Familiar voices drift up:
Sweetpea exploring the beams
of a high-rise while Popeye and Bluto fight
over who will be the rescuer.

He sweeps the binoculars back to where
the towboat *Daniel J* (he's kept a log
since moving here with his mother)
vanishes around a bend. He hears
his name now but wants to finish
the illustrated story of a boy

in Micronesia, a pearl diver
who frightens his father by riding
a manta ray. Spiraling in joy
off the edge of a reef, will he let go
and surface grinning beside the boat?

RAG RUGS

From attics and cedar chests,
from rummage sales and remnant stores,
clothing comes in charity
to an old woman who knows the values
of light and dark, weave and weight,
braiding them into her livelihood—
patchwork, banded, calico, all displayed
along the railing of her front porch.
Today a boy working on a merit badge
pumps wobbling up her steep street,
the basket on his bicycle filled.

She is finishing an oval,
lacing the plaited lengths together
with her needle curved like a tiny rib.
Unfolding what he's brought, she wants
to show him the steps.
Pockets, collars, zippers unstitch
and seams come open, then
she cuts the fabric into strips,
sorting them on the parlor floor.
Shuttling among the choices there,
she braids three strands at once
in a rhythm reaching through
the outgrown and out-of-fashion, while he
imagines coasting the whole way back.

Looking at him she thinks of her own son,
his Radio Flyer wagon and its route
in 1943. What swaying stacks of old newspapers
(cartoon mice with Tojo's face),
what pyramids of tin cans flashing
victory up and down this hill—
but he died in the next war.

This boy working on a merit badge
has to leave before dark, but first
she brings him into the herb garden
and clips a sampling he'll carry home.
They have their virtues, these varieties
her son found in a bombed-out monastery
on his unit's long march from the Yalu.
He copied this out for her:
Hail be thou holie herbs,
All on the Mount of Calvarie
Thou didst first appear.
Thou art good for manie a sore
And healest manie a wound.
In the name of sweet Jesus
I take thee from the ground.

She says nothing of him,
but writes on slips of paper
that fennel makes an unguent against fever
while costmary calms a hornet sting
and sorrel toughens the teeth.
Then she lets the boy go,
in the basket of his bicycle some curatives
from a letter full of seeds.

High Season

A squall over open water, gray
rainfall like a bundle of cut stalks,
becomes a root mass, dangling,
clods of black scud before the wind:

no sky at all for the time-share
villas. It washes free a bone or two
in crossing an uninhabited

scrub cay a mile offshore, where
Arawak Indians who would not
labor in the gold mines of the Crown
or pay tribute—a falcon's bell

full of gold dust from riverbeds—
lay tethered by wrist and ankle
to rods anchored in rock. Before

sails blazoned the cross of Castile
among the islands, Arawaks
had different words for rain falling
on a volcano's boiling vents,

on stone carvings of gods, on root crops,
but no word for what fell on wounds
from flogging and the teeth of wolfhounds.

The squall moves off, keeping to sea
and taking with it the New World,
those flags and caravels and mines.
The cay's tall navigation light comes on.

CREEK FIRE

Watching the kids' swing flail and curl
in disembodied patterns on its long ropes
clinched to an oak limb, I saw

the basketball hoop on the trunk glow
with a blue corona like a gas burner:
St. Elmo's Fire, then lightning,

and when I opened my eyes again
that balancing of charged fields
had brought the tree down.

All night as lines of thunderstorms
came through, the counts between flash and pulse
dropping out, the oak's crown

lay bank to bank in the creek
along our property line. Morning,
and the tree's come back in this fall current

as miscellany of a year upstream—
so many leaves they obscure the branches,
like monarch butterflies on a swarming tree.

Sycamore, maple, beech. One time
a gang of us found drums of kerosene
behind the abandoned Amoco and aimed

arcs into a stream at the edge of town.
We gave that slick a head start
before touching it off, kept up with the flames

a while, shaking leaves down to see them
spurt like match heads,
then hid while firemen pounded brooms

at blazing weeds along the banks.
Ash and the odor of smoke
kept their secret in our sweaters and hair.

LATE WINTER IN A FIELD

These redbuds along the creek,
their leaves are pure
inwardness, unbroken buds,

nothing yet to take the place
of leaves lost to the bottom
of that pool below the rapids.
Still, on every limb

pink-to-crimson blossoms loft
keel and banner and wings.
Although a certain tint

that overwintered in moss
is on the move and closing
on bunch grass like umbrellas
blown inside out, mistiming

is one lesson a field
learns over and over. Redbuds
want every risk to flower.

River Changes

Though woods undercut at the island's
blunt upstream end affirm
how current carries the day,
silt and seeds come together
at the tapering lower tip
where goldenrod hold and deepen
the new earth, their stems bulbous
with gall midges wintering over.
The river sends word ahead:
by papery-winged fruits
and catkins like scraps of batting
the familiar comes back to be known
over and over, beginning
This is what happened . . .
and the island goes by, taking root.

THE CASSAVA WOMEN

Hispaniola, ca. 1600

Climbing switchbacks into the cloud forest,
men come with basketfuls of cassava
root, and the ancients of the island
are waiting, who have it from the gods
how to make themselves worthy:
drinking the milkbush's bitter sap
turns breath, catarrh, teeth, as poisonous
as cassava itself. Essences war
then cancel each other to a purity
as these women chew their way through
the root harvest, letting fall a spume
into rainwater, a savor the men
age in a still-house to deepen
its reach. After bowing all day
to fields like sea surges over their heads,
cane harvesters drink it and witness
the gods of hurricanes and starlight,
hearthfire and childbirth, as they were
before caravels changed the horizon.
Souls the color of volcanic sand are
lost forever, the friars preach, without
forgiveness that arrived with the cross
of Castile on sails in the anchorage.
But cassava women know how their souls
go on from them. Not long ago,
coming upon the still-house of slaves
down a dim unplantable gulley
on his property, the master pulled out
the rag bung of a cask then brought
his candle too close. Whereupon
the old ones' breath flew out and seized the flame
and ruffled silken arm that held it.

GRIMES GOLDEN

John filled my lap with wild columbine
the April morning we left Independence,
and by noon I learned how women gather
away from the Trail to unpleat their
long skirts and screen one another.

A month later, cloud shadows bending
across the prairie's ridges and swales
like gull wings, a grave appeared
like none we had ever found.
While children sang in a ring around
a cottonwood, our wagonmaster pointed out
how someone had axed the trunk hollow
—cholera? childbirth?—then sealed it
with a limestone slab against wolves.

That night a dance and minstrel show,
a tall spree of tambourine and flute,
till at last I fell asleep quilting
a pattern of apples, the very ones
in our deed to acreage in Oregon.

Oh, the men won't let me go back
to where they closed John up in a tree.
Will the roots hold? Will fire avoid him?
The eleventh of June, 1852, and I
was stitching an apple, a Grimes Golden.
Unyoking our oxen, he called out
for me to notice Chimney Rock ahead,
called out we'd carve our names there . . .
then went down under the hoofs.

The men have put the reins in my hands.
A week now, straight into the wind.

The grasses bowing as I pass,
do they wish me well?

I knew John's law from the start.
Nothing worth less than a dollar a pound
could be given room, yet I hid
bags of seed from my flower garden.
"Who are you?" says the Grimes Golden.

My mind fills with rootings, annuals
and perennials, their stems moving
through furniture, tools, utensils,
their blossoms crowding under sailcloth
so I can hardly breathe
or cry out, *I am Esther Pennell*,
or see the Trail happening before me
in its penitence of yokes.